W9-CKT-379
3 2711 00092 6885

Requiem for New Orleans

DATE DUE

NOV 1 6 2006		
DEC 1 2 2007		
APR 1 6 2008		

2006

Demco, Inc. 38-293

COLUMBIA COLLEGE LIBRARY
600 S. MICHIGAN AVENUE
CHICAGO, IL 60605

Requiem for New Orleans

Mike Sharpe

NORTH CASTLE BOOKS
An imprint of M.E.Sharpe, INC.

Copyright © 2006 by Mike Sharpe

All rights reserved. No part of this book may be reproduced in any form
without written permission from the publisher, M.E. Sharpe, Inc.,
80 Business Park Drive, Armonk, New York 10504.

North Castle Books is an imprint of M.E. Sharpe, Inc.

Library of Congress Cataloging-in-Publication Data

Sharpe, Mike, 1928-
    Requiem for New Orleans / Mike Sharpe.
      p. cm.
    ISBN 0-7656-1766-8 (pbk. : alk. paper)
    1. New Orleans (La.)--Poetry. I. Title.

PS3619.H35665R47 2006
    811'.6--dc22   2005036587

Printed in the United States of America

The paper used in this publication meets the minimum requirements of
American National Standard for Information Sciences
Permanence of Paper for Printed Library Materials,
ANSI Z 39.48-1984.

BM (p)   10   9   8   7   6   5   4   3   2   1

Again
To my wife Carole.

To my children,
Susanna, Matthew, Elisabeth, and Hana

Welcome, tourists
Welcome to The Big Easy USA
We hope your hotel accommodations are comfortable
We hope you enjoy your stay
Your admission tickets include all the dioramas
and all the rides
Don't miss the daily Mardi Gras parade
Or the gourmet cooking and the mellow jazz
The French Quarter is fully restored
Take a walk down by the levee
Welcome to The Big Easy USA
Just like New Orleans used to be

Contents

I Requiem

Requiem aeternam dona eis, Domine
Et lux perpetua luceat eis

Rest these bodies floating in the water
Rest these bodies lying in rooms
Rest these bodies washed into bayous

Grant them eternal rest, O Lord
And may light eternal shine upon them

Rest the old and young abandoned to die

II New Orleans, Where Do You Come From?

I come from Indians, Africans, French, Spanish, English, Cajuns, Creoles, Irish, Catholics, Protestants, Jews, Voodoos. I come from the high and the low.

I come from the Mississippi. I come from barges and ships. I come from cargo. Grain, cotton, oil, tobacco. Timber and steel. I come from revelers and gamblers and crooks. From whores and pirates and slaves. I come from corruption and sin and graft. I come from musicians, artists, writers, longshoremen, sailors, and oilmen. Lawyers and clergymen too. Bartenders, hotel keepers, and restauranteurs. From women working all kinds of places behind the scenes. I come from the upscale and the lowdown. I come from master man and slave woman. I am Mardi Gras parades. And blues. I am jazz.

I got a lot of streets and places to go. I got men to build levees. I got men to move barges. I got men to haul garbage. I got ladies to make beds and cook and clean and take care of kids. I got boys to say yes ma'am, yes sir, anything you want, sir. I got men who will take your pocketbook and take your life. I got men who will blow a horn and stir your soul.

Oh, New Orleans, you fishbowl, city below the sea, gumbo pot, pleasure spot, you free and easy, you lurid lowlife, you race mixer, you masquerade, you down and out, you high and mighty, you dive of all sorts and kinds. Shacks, mansions, bars, parks, churches of your choice, spicy food places. Run-down schools. Easy-going folks. Men on the prowl. Tourists, walk in groups.

Have you ever been to New Orleans?
It's the hottest thing you've ever seen.

When you're feeling down and out
and you feel there's no way out
tell them drop me off in New Orleans.
So drop me off in New Orleans.
Drop me off in New Orleans.

III Katrina

Well, New Orleans wore a great big mask
Then the winds began to blow.
And the water came rushing in.
The mask blew off and we had to go.

Well, New Orleans was a beautiful town.
New Orleans was a rocking place.
Then the winds began to blow
And we had no other place to go.

No place to go.
No buses to take us there.

Mr. President, come on down and help us out.

Katrina can't help herself.
Katrina's got no brain.
The President, he's got a brain.
But the wheels don't spin too very fast.

Katrina, she can't care.
The President, yeah, he can care.
But he don't care too very much.
Yeah, he don't care to save New Orleans.
He's got bigger things to think about.
Iraq, Iran, and such.

4

He looked away, he looked away.
He looked away from the levees.
He looked away from the floods.
He looked away from the houses.
He looked away from New Orleans.
And his mask blew off with the wind.

He looked away as the levees breached.
He looked away as the waters rushed in.
He looked away as New Orleans pleaded.
He's got bigger things on his mind.
Iraq, Iran, and such.

Well, come on down and ride your bike past the rotting corpses and
the living dead.
Past the splintered houses and the fade-out memories.
Come on down and ride your bike
Past the rotting corpses and the living dead
And the fade-out memories.

Mr. President in Washington
His mask was blown away.
What will you do when the winds blow again
And the waters rush in?
What will you do when the levees give way
And your mask blows off with the wind?

Well, there's stinking bodies floating in the water
and stinking bodies lying in rooms.
There's stinking bodies at the doorways
and stinking bodies in the attics.
There's corpses in the chapels too
and dead swept away in the bayou.

It's Judgment Day in my court.
I'm speaking to you, Mr. President of the United States.
It's Judgment Day in my court.

Requiem aeternam dona eis, Domine
Et lux perpetua luceat eis.

Grant them eternal rest, O Lord
And may light eternal shine upon them.

Rest the bodies floating in the water.
Rest the bodies in rooms.
Rest the bodies at doorways.
Rest the corpses in the attics.
Rest the dead in the chapels too
and those swept away in the bayou.

IV Stay Back

And they mocked and said:
You can't come over the bridge
You can't come over the bridge
And they mocked and said:
You can't come over the bridge
You can't come over the bridge.
They took our food, they took our water
And they shot their guns over our heads.
And they mocked and said:
You can't come over the bridge.

Doctor went to Louisiana to see what he could see.
Doctor, turn around, no use to wait.
You don't have a license to practice in this state.

Had a load of ice in my truck.
Headed for New Orleans to help those out of luck.
Got to New Orleans told to go to Biloxi.
Went to Biloxi told to go to Baton Rouge.
Went to Baton Rouge told to go to New Orleans.
Headed for New Orleans to help those out of luck.
No more ice left in my truck.

Pilots of a Navy plane
detoured to New Orleans
and rescued one hundred and ten.
Commander of the mission
reprimanded his men.
Follow my orders
don't detour again.

Three students from Duke
Drove down to New Orleans.
Guard at the bridge said stop your car.
Students thought what shall we do.
Made up press passes
Rolled right on through.
Made two trips to Baton Rouge.
Saved seven people in all.
Three kids in a Hyundai
Moved people out of town.
And the National Guard isn't around?
Isn't there something wrong?
What made them take so long?

Woman waves shirt at helicopter above.
Shouts, hey guys, six on this roof.
In the sun, beginning to roast.
No food or water for four long days.
Father, Son, and Holy Ghost.
They flew right over us.
Can hold out another day at most.

We crossed the bridge and the policeman said
Get out of the bus and lie down on the ground
Cursed at us for being black and brown
Now get back on the bus and get out of town
You're not welcome here so don't stick around.

The word was spread. If you want to be safe, go to the Convention Center and the Superdome.

But the power went out, the toilets overflowed, it stinks like hell in here. Children crying, old people dying, the temperature is up to 110. We can't take it anymore, we have to get out of here. I'm saying, we have to get out of here.

Isn't anybody listening? We have to get out of here.

> *I gotta right to sing the blues*
> *I gotta right to feel low down*
> *And I gotta right to hang around*
> *Down by the river, oh yeah.*

V In Iraq

Where are you, my darling soldier
Where are you, my darling boy?

I'm in Iraq, mother, I'm in Iraq.

I'm drowning, my darling soldier
I'm drowning, my darling boy.

I can't reach you, mother dear.
I can't reach you.
I'm over here, mother, I'm over here.

Goodbye, my darling soldier
Goodbye, my darling boy.

Goodbye, mother, goodbye mother. Goodbye.

Where are you, my darling mother,
Where are you, my darling dear?

I'm in New Orleans, son, I'm in New Orleans.

I'm dying, my darling mother
I'm dying, my darling dear.

I can't reach you, my lovely son.
I can't reach you.
I'm over here, son, I'm over here.

Goodbye, my darling mother
Goodbye, my darling dear.

Goodbye, son, goodbye son. Goodbye.

VI Death

We walk among the bodies, the stench, you and I walk . . .
I have come for you. I care.
You poor, you black. I give you preferential treatment
never given in life.
Black women, I give you preferential treatment.
Little babies, I give you preferential treatment.
You poor and sick, I give you preferential treatment.
I am here to help.

I visit the hospitals, I visit the houses, I visit the doomed city.
I care about you.
I take care of the poor, the outcasts.
The last in line shall be first.
I cannot bear the heat. I cannot bear the stench. Come with me in
the cool shade.
Come with me.
Come with me.

VII Where Are You, God?

I am poor and black
abandoned
abandoned all my life.

I am poor and white
abandoned
abandoned all my life.

Where are you, God?
Where is my salvation?

I wonder if they that mourn are blessed:
I wonder if they shall be comforted.

I wonder if the meek are blessed:
I wonder if they shall inherit the earth.

I wonder if, when men revile me,
and persecute me, and say all manner
of evil against me, I am blessed.

I wonder if I ask, it shall be given me.
I wonder if I seek, I shall find.
I wonder if I knock, it shall be opened to me.

Dies irae, dies illa,
Quantus tremor est futurus,
Quando judex est venturus
cuncta stricte discussurus!

This day, this day of wrath,
What trembling there shall be,
When the judge shall come
To weigh everything strictly!

Where are you, God?
Where are you?
You say you are merciful, but I have not received mercy.
You say you are just, but I have not received justice.
You say the door is open, but I have not been allowed to come in.
Creator, what have you created?
Where are you?

You are not my shepherd;
I am in want.
You do not allow me to lie down in green pastures;
You do not restore my soul.
Yea, I walk through the valley of the shadow of death.
I fear evil: for thou art not with me.

*I am the Lord thy God. Do not despair in the
darkness.
I am all that you have dreamed.
Look around.
Look, Man and Woman, to the earth as well as
heaven.
Man, Woman, what have you created?
You who have tilled the land.
You who have built cities.
You who have become cunning.
You who have lifted up the mighty though he be a
grain of sand among ten thousand.
I gave you the earth, you who are ten thousand many
times over.
Look around you.
Look within you.
Look and see what you have dreamed.
You who have become cunning.
You who have lifted up the mighty though he be a
grain of sand among ten thousand.
Look around you.
Look within you.
Look and see what you have dreamed.
Man, Woman, abandon not yourselves.
Listen not to honeyed words.
What have you created from what I have created?*

Hear my answer, O God.

I who was perplexed and deceived.

My reproach is idle.

I judge and reproach myself.

Nor am I a grain of sand blown in the wind.

I who was ignorant will help my neighbor and say:

Do not despair in the darkness.

Look and see what we have dreamed.

We will rebuild the levees.

We will rebuild the houses.

We will beautify the city with heart-chords of music and sway-
rhythms of dance.

We will awaken from a deep sleep

And look into ourselves

And remember what we have dreamed.

We will awaken from a deep sleep

And remember what we have dreamed.

VIII Entr'acte, Part 1: Walking on the Sunny Side of the Street

Quote:

"I believe the town [New Orleans] where I used to come from Houston, Texas, to enjoy myself – occasionally too much – will be that very same town, that it will be a better place to come to."

— George W. Bush, Houston, September 9, 2005

Quote:

"This is working out very well for them. And so many people in the arena here, you know, were underprivileged anyway, so this – this is working very well for them."

— Barbara Bush on tour of hurricane relief centers in Houston, September 5, 2005

Quote:

"I don't think anyone anticipated the break in the levees."

— George W. Bush, September 1, 2005

Quote:

"That 'perfect storm' of a combination of catastrophes exceeded the foresight of the planners, and maybe anyone's foresight."

— Michael Chertoff, Secretary of Homeland Security, September 5, 2005

Quote:

"Considering the dire circumstances that we have in New Orleans, virtually a city that has been destroyed, things are going relatively well."

> — Michael D. Brown, Director of the Federal Emergency Management Agency, September 2, 2005

Quote:

"You're doing a heck of a job, Brownie."

> — George W. Bush, about Michael D. Brown, at the time of the flooding of New Orleans

Entr'acte, Part 2:
. . . and on the Shady Side of the Street

Quote:

"We certainly understood the potential impact of a Category 4 or 5 hurricane."

> — Lt. General Carl Strock, chief of engineers for the
> US Army Corps of Engineers, September 1, 2005

Quote:

". . . A major hurricane could decimate the region, but flooding from even a moderate storm could kill thousands. It's just a matter of time . . ."

> —*New Orleans Times-Picayune*, June 2002

Quote:

"New Orleans was the No. 1 disaster we were talking about. We were obsessed with New Orleans because of the risk."

> — Eric L. Tolbert, a top FEMA official, January 2005

Quote:

"We know what needs to be done and then we turn around and don't fund it."

> — Mike Parker, former assistant secretary of the Army,
> who left office in 2002 when funding for the
> Army Corps of Engineers was cut.

Quote:

"This is a desperate SOS. Right now we are out of resources at the Convention Center and don't anticipate enough buses. Currently the Convention Center is unsanitary and we are running out of supplies for 15,000 to 20,000 people."

—Mayor Ray Nagin, September 2, 2005

Quote:

"Have any of you here seen my kids?"

— William Cousins, September 2, 2005

IX Diaspora

Dear William:

I'm with the lost people
Sitting on beds
Lined up in rows
Lying under covers
Talking with strangers
Watching TV
Taking care of kids.

I'm with the lost people
In a strange place
People talking
People walking
Babies crying
Old men sighing.

I'm with the lost people at the store
Hair brushes and lip balm
Towels and soap
All kinds of things
No need to pay
Haven't got a nickel anyway.

I have food and water
A roof over my head
A place to lie down in bed

They can't give me what I need most.

I'm with the lost people
I want to know
Where are my children
Where are my friends
Where is my house
Where is my man.

I'm with the lost people
Back in New Orleans
In my dreams
I don't know –
No place we can go
Waiting around in a strange town
Is getting me down.

I'm with the lost people
I'm feeling weary and I'm feeling blue
I suppose you're feeling that way too.

I'll mail you this letter
When I get your address.

Your ever loving
Bess

What happens to a dream deferred?
Does it fester, does it dry up, does it stink?

Does it yank you back?

What happens to a dream deferred?
The waters come rushing in.

Will the waters cleanse America's name?
Or will America stay just the same?

X *Preamble to the Constitution*

We the people of the United States, in order to form a more perfect union, ESTABLISH DOMESTIC TRANQUILITY, PROVIDE FOR THE COMMON DEFENSE, PROMOTE THE GENERAL WELFARE, AND SECURE THE BLESSINGS OF LIBERTY FOR OURSELVES AND OUR POSTERITY, do ordain and establish this Constitution for the United States of America.

Does this mean that the President, the Congress, and the Supreme Court have a responsibility to THE WHOLE COUNTRY?

Does this mean that the United States is a COMMUNITY?

Does this mean that the general welfare is the welfare of EVERYBODY?

Does this mean that the blessings of liberty imply some kind of EQUALITY?

Does this mean that domestic tranquility requires the government to repair levees so A WHOLE CITY WON'T BE WASHED AWAY?

While the scholars debate:

> *Stay back, little children, stay back.*
> *Stay back little children*
> *If you haven't got the fare.*
>
> *Stay back, grown up folks, stay back.*
> *Stay back grown up folks*
> *If you haven't got the fare.*

24

XI Jeremiah in New Orleans

Eicha yashva vadad ha-ir
Rabati am
Hay-ta k'almana;
Rabati vagoyim
Sarati bam'dinot
Hay'ta lamas.

How does the city sit solitary
That was full of people.
How has she become as a widow.
She that was great among the nations
And princess among the provinces,
How is she become tributary!

She weepeth sore in the night,
And her tears are on her cheeks.
She hath none to comfort her
Among all the mighty.
All the mighty have dealt treacherously with her,
They are become her enemies.

The mighty wander as blind men on the street,
They are polluted with blood
So that men cannot touch their garments.
Depart, ye unclean! They cried unto them.
Depart, depart! touch us not . . .

XII A Dream and an Awakening

My name is William, I am from New Orleans. Who's that coming into my room?

I'm the President of the United States.

You are not welcome. You have given me much grief. It is best that you go.

Wait. Hear what I say. God appeared to me this very night in a dream, saying:

You are mighty.

You can restore cities.

You can lift up the poor.

You can assuage the sorrow of mothers.

You can comfort fathers.

You can ease the suffering of the sick and the aged.

You can find work for those who languish idly.

You can bring peace to the world.

I heard God's true message.

I abjure false voices.

As God has forgiven me, can you not also forgive me?

I forgive, I forgive. Who am I, holier than God, that I cannot forgive?

I have to go, William, and do my work. Count on me. I'll come again.

William woke up and sat up in bed. Ah God! How could I dream such stupid stuff? Goddamn my wretched dream. Goddamn this run-down trailer. Goddamn this run-down camp. Goddamn me far from home. Goddamn me sitting by myself. Goddamn you, Mr. President of the United States of America, for messing with my dream.

The spotlight came on
And the President said
And the President said
And the President said
And those without stayed without
When the spotlight went out.

And they wandered and they wandered
And they couldn't come home
They crouched like beasts
in run-down shacks
No place to go, no place to go

Goodbye, New Orleans
Goodbye, New Orleans
We can't come home
No place to go, no place to go

Started out low
Ended up low
No place to go, no place to go

Which way out for me, America
Which way out?
You cry for me, America,
You cry for me

Which way out for me, America
Which way out for me?
Which way out for you and me, America
Which way out for you and me?

Mors stupebit et natura,
Cum resurget creatura,
Iudicanti responsura.

Liber scriptus proferetur,
In quo totum continetur,
Unde mundus judicetur.

Death and nature shall be stunned
When mankind arises
to render account before the judge.

The written book shall be brought,
In which all is contained,
Whereby the world shall be judged.

When   will   that   be?

Postscript

The Requiem Mass for the dead is a Latin text transformed into a universal statement by Bach, Mozart, Berlioz, Verdi, Fauré, and numerous other composers. I take it as a statement of universal lament and so the title for these ruminations.

I hear *Requiem for New Orleans* as a symphony with narrator, soloists, chorus, and orchestra, with muscular and lyrical passages interrupted by clanging dissonances, derived from biblical cadences, black idiom, standard American speech, jazz, and the caustic side of modern composers like Shostakovich and Bernstein.

The climax of *Requiem for New Orleans* is a conversation between a man and God or a woman and God. I do not intend the conversation to be read in a literal sense but rather as a colloquy between a thinking person and his or her conscience. Religion in a literal sense, or in a figurative sense, as I intend it, invokes solemnity as no other attitude can, no matter what a person's belief or disbelief. The destruction of New Orleans cannot be discussed in any way except with solemnity. The destruction of New Orleans is the first time that an entire city – almost an entire city – has been wiped out in the United States, many of its inhabitants killed, and the rest turned into refugees in their own country. The biblical proportions are manifest.

I said that the destruction of New Orleans must be discussed with solemnity. I do not contradict myself when I say that it must be discussed with scorn as well as solemnity, solemn scorn. New Orleans was not destroyed by a hurricane but by abandonment: abandonment of responsibility to protect the city; abandonment of responsibility to save the people; abandonment by leaders who speak compassionately but do not act in accordance with their words. *Requiem for New*

Orleans is a tapestry of bereavement and scorn, the strands woven together as our conscience is woven together, in a bewildering pattern.

The climax that I refer to occurs in Section VII, entitled "Where Are You, God?" which appears as an accusation against God, but which is an expression of doubt about our own ability to overcome human-created tragedy. God replies as a revolutionary: The answer is up to you. The answer depends on what you do. The penitent speaker then acknowledges that human-imposed tragedy is not the work of God but of humans. Humans, not God, are responsible for rescuing themselves.

"Stay Back" (Section IV) describes not only racism, but a rule-bound rigidity that kept doctors out of Louisiana, ice trucks running from city to city (and trucks with other supplies as well), Navy commanders so hide-bound that they could not tolerate initiative to save the drowning, the thirsting, and the starving. The failed roof-scene rescue is not an indictment of the National Guard, but of the failure of leadership to anticipate the magnitude of the disaster. "Stay Back," like the entire *Requiem,* is an indictment of the ineptness, disorganization, and circus-barker aura of our self-congratulating leaders in Washington. The "rescue" of New Orleans is very, very low burlesque.

New Orleans had many heroes. I write about three students from Duke University (Section IV) who could not sit still and watch a tragedy from the sidelines. Their actions can be multiplied by the thousands.

The "Diaspora" (Section IX) is such an immense phenomenon that I use two incidents to stand in for the whole. One is an imaginary letter written by a woman taking refuge at the Austin Convention Center, based on observations of my daughter, Susanna, who worked at the Center as a volunteer. The other is an imaginary incident, a dream and an awakening (Section XII).

No writing could evoke the betrayal of New Orleans with such bitterness as The Lamentations of Jeremiah over the fate of Jerusalem (Section XI), and this after the passage of 2650 years. The similarities astound me. Will we now learn to be civilized and finish with the destruction of cities, and now the planet, once and for all?

New Orleans was an American treasure of people, history, language, music, dance, cuisine, architecture, industry and ambience washed away in one day by human inaction. George Bush and his crew stood by as onlookers as this treasure was destroyed. In a flash we saw the collapse of the Bush government. We can mock the circus of incompetence, but incompetence is only a symptom of a deeper disorder. The deeper disorder is the belief that our central government is only a spectator to the travails of citizens and that it is up to the citizens to take care of themselves; that the White House is not the headquarters of a national insurance company; that the idea of a community of mutual help is as dead as the New Deal. For years we've heard that government gets in the way. After one stormy day, we learned – *it ain't necessarily so*. We speak of failed states in Africa, the Middle East, and southern Asia. Why look so far away?

If *Requiem for New Orleans* is ambiguous, let it be. I am writing about ambiguity. If life and death jostle one another, let it be told just as it is. For a moment, a light on New Orleans lit up a third world country within a first world country.

A Note on Quotations and Acknowledgments

Several passages in *Requiem for New Orleans* are quotations. *These passages are in italic type.*

1. The lines in Latin and English on pages 1 and 6 are from the Requiem Mass.

2. The lines on page 3 are from the song, "Drop Me Off in New Orleans," by Kermit Ruffins. Copyright © Kermit Ruffins.

3. The lines on page 9 are from the song, "I Gotta Right to Sing the Blues," words by Ted Koehler, music by Harold Arlen. Copyright © 1932 (renewed) Warner Brothers, Inc. All rights reserved. Used by permission.

4. The lines on pages 14 and 28 in Latin and English are from the "Dies Irae" (Days of Wrath) section of the Requiem Mass.

5. The line on page 23, "What happens to a dream deferred," is from *Harlem* by Langston Hughes.

6. The lines on page 24 are an inversion of the Negro folk song, "Get on Board Little Children."

7. The passages in Hebrew and English on page 25 are from the "Lamentations of Jeremiah."

8. The italic paragraph on page 15 is *not* from any source but is original with the author.

9. The item on three students from Duke University on page 8 is based on a news story by Ian Urbina, *The New York Times,* September 19, 2005.

10. The inspiration for the letter on pages 21–22 came from an e-mail sent to family and friends by my daughter Susanna Sharpe, who spent September 11, 2005, as a Red Cross volunteer at the Austin Convention Center.

11. The William referred to in sections VIII, IX, and XII is fictitious. The question on page 20, "Have any of you here seen my kids?" is based on news reports from the Superdome.

The Future of New Orleans

I wrote *Requiem for New Orleans* in September and October, 2005. Katrina bore down on New Orleans August 28. The levees were breached August 29, inundating 80 percent of the city. Help from the federal government arrived September 2. A second hurricane, Rita, hit the city on September 23, exacerbating the damage.

Almost 450,000 New Orlinians scattered all over the United States, particularly Louisiana, Mississippi, and Texas. Some large, unknown numbers are not going back because they have no incentive to go back and no place to go back to. The old New Orleans will never be the old New Orleans again because most of the residents won't be there. No matter how passionately New Orlinians want old New Orleans back, they can't have it.

This great out-migration is accompanied by nature's aggression. New Orleans is sinking and the oceans are rising. In thirty years most of the city will be more than 20 feet below sea level. The heart-broken New Orlininans who have come back, or who want to come back, say: Press on. Rebuild levees; reconfigure canals along the Mississippi so that silt can be carried downstream and restore barrier islands; construct a sea gate; let the marshes regenerate; build better pumping stations; plan a middle class city. New Orleans has given so much to America; it's time for America to give to New Orleans.

But skeptical politicians and some very unpopular geologists and hydrologists ask, why spend tens of billions on a sinking city when they can be spent on solid ground? Why not a more modest New Orleans on the 20 percent of the land above sea level and invest those tens of billions where nature is on our side?

I do not know what the future of New Orleans will be nor does anyone else. One grotesque possibility is described in the epigraph of this book: Theme Park New Orleans. Other grotesque possibilities can be imagined. Our political class will undoubtedly imagine them and pursue several at the same time. I wrote, "We will rebuild the levees." This must be taken as a metaphor that refers to the entire country.

Also Available from North Castle Books

Spartacus
Howard Fast
" . . . Fast's pages take on a brilliance." – *The New York Times Book Review*

Winner of the American Library Association's Notable Book Award
The Hessian
The Classic Novel with a New Foreword
Howard Fast
"Moving in its simplicity and directness." – *Publishers Weekly*

The Last Frontier A New Edition with a Special Introduction by the Author
Howard Fast
"A rich American novel." – *The New York Times Book Review*

A Brief History of American Culture
Robert M. Crunden
"A readable, insightful overview of the underlying patterns that give shape to
U.S. cultural history." – *Booklist*

American Space, Jewish Time: *Essays in Modern Culture and Politics*
Stephen J. Whitfield
"Whitfield's intellectual scope, ready wit, and sparkling style make this book
a pure pleasure." – *American Jewish History*

Through the Moral Maze: *Searching for Absolute Values in a Pluralistic World*
Robert Kane
"A penetrating look into the erosion of Western values." – *The Beacon* (UK)

Thou Shalt Not Kill Unless Otherwise Instructed: *Poems and Stories*
Mike Sharpe
"A people's poet praying for an end to 9/11 by making 9/11 unforgettable."
– Governor Mario M. Cuomo

Children of the Paper Crane: *The Story of Sadako Sasaki and Her Struggle
with the A-Bomb Disease*
Masamoto Nasu; Translated by Elizabeth W. Baldwin, Steven L. Leeper,
and Kyoko Yoshida
"A beautiful and moving biography." – *Booklist*

Chinese Folktales: *An Anthology*
Translated by Yin-lien C. Chin, Yetta S. Center, and Mildred Ross
"Flows with the naturalness of conversation."– *The Small Press Book Review*

Shamanic Worlds: *Rituals and Lore of Siberia and Central Asia*
Edited by Marjorie Mandelstam Balzer
". . . a welcome addition to our meager understanding of shamanism on that
side of the world." –*Shaman's Drum*

Selected Titles in Literature from M.E. Sharpe

Freedom Road A New Ed. with Primary Documents and Intro. by Eric Foner
Howard Fast
" . . . a high-geared story, told with that peculiar dramatic intensity of which
Fast is a master." – *Chicago Daily News*

**An Anthology of Russian Literature from Earliest Writings to Modern
Fiction:** *Introduction to a Culture.* Includes an interactive multimedia CD
Edited by Nicholas Rzhevsky
"One of the most comprehensive anthologies of Russian literature in English
ever published." – *British East-West Journal*

Land of Exile: *Contemporary Korean Fiction*
Ed. and trans. by Marshall R. Pihl, Bruce Fulton, and Ju-Chan Fulton
"Shatters the mold in which Korean literature has thus far been presented to
the West." – *New Asia Review*

Peace Under Heaven: *A Modern Korean Novel*
Man-Sik Ch'ae; Translated by Chun Kyung-Ja
"A brilliant black comedy from Korea's colonial past, *Peace Under Heaven* is
at once grotesque, funny, sad and universally appealing."
        – Carter Eckert, Harvard University

My Very Last Possession: *And Other Stories by Pak Wanso*
Pak Wanso; Translated by Chun Kyung-Ja
"Discloses for the American reader the range of one of South Korea's most
distinguished living writers." – *Publishers Weekly*

By the winner of the 1994 Nobel Prize for Literature
The Pinch Runner Memorandum
Ōe Kenzaburo; Translated by Michiko N. Wilson and Michael K. Wilson
"A heartening display of the explosively constructive power of imagination."
        – *The New Yorker*

The Woman with the Flying Head and Other Stories
Kurahashi Yumiko; Edited and translated by Atsuko Sakaki
"Her fantastic, often erotic characters challenge our notions about rationality,
sexual identity and the relationship of body and mind." – *The New York Times*

Silk and Insight *(Kinu to Meisatsu): A Novel*
Yukio Mishima; Edited by Frank Gibney; Translated by Hiroaki Sato
"A container for the poetic insights of a great literary master of our time."
        – *The Japan Times*

Everyone and Everything in Trollope *(4 volumes)*
Edited by George Newlin
"An essential addition to major research collections in literature and Victorian
studies." – *American Reference Books Annual*

For more information visit www.mesharpe.com

Photo by Liz Sharpe

Mike Sharpe has written widely on economics, politics, and world affairs, and is the author of *John Kenneth Galbraith and the Lower Economics*. He worked with Senators Humphrey and Javits to draft The Full Employment and Balanced Growth Act of 1978 and was economic advisor to Senator Birch Bayh in his bid for the presidency. He is founder and president of M.E. Sharpe publishing company. His collection *Thou Shalt Not Kill Unless Otherwise Instructed: Poems and Stories* was published by North Castle Books in 2005.